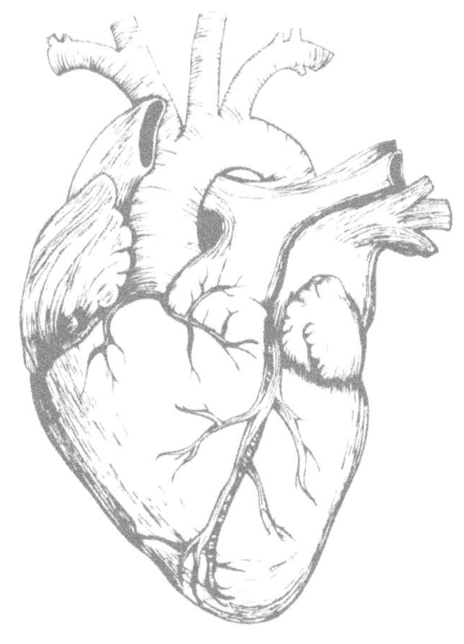

K -

thank you for helping me find my voice.

Emani -

love always always always.

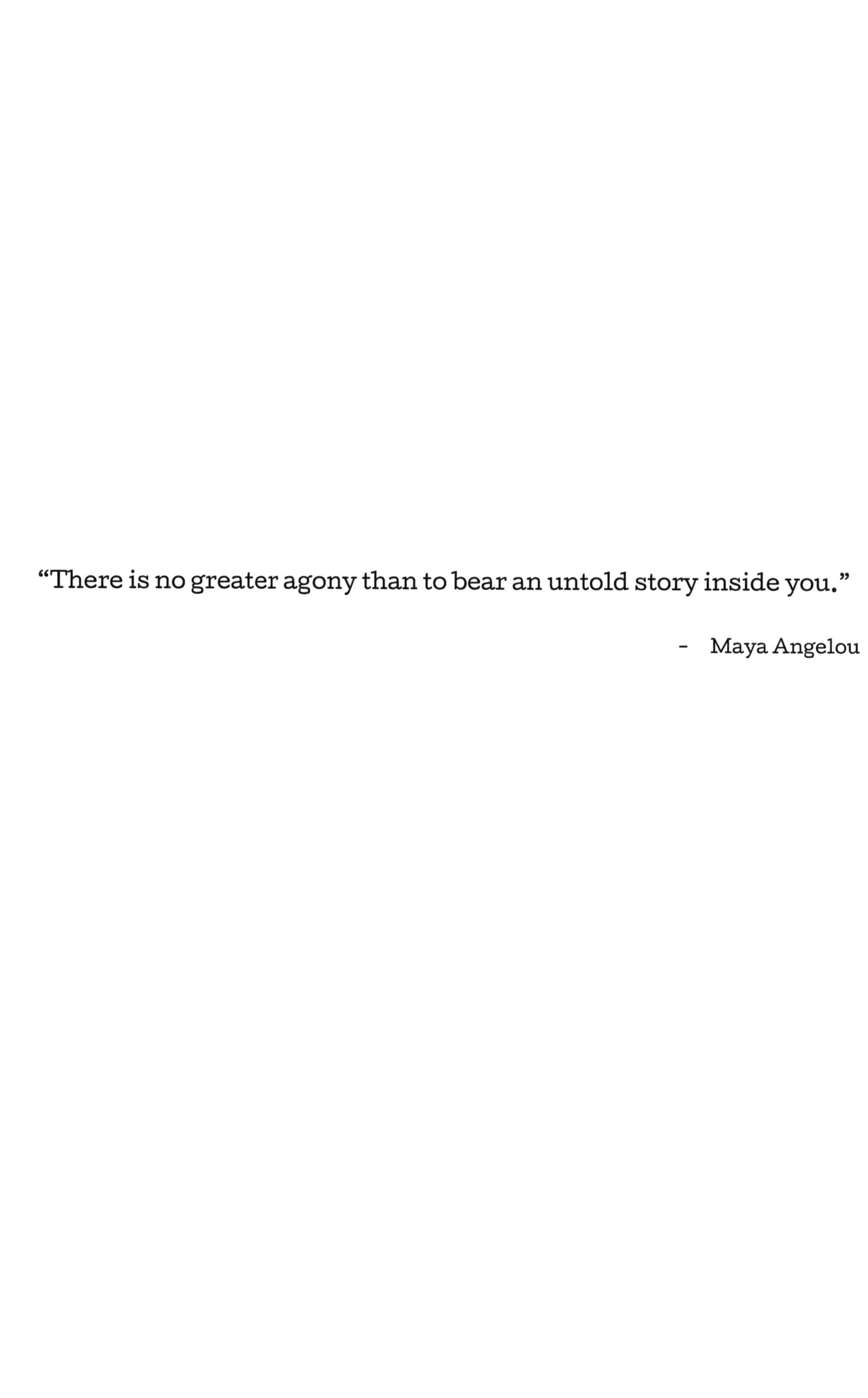

"There is no greater agony than to bear an untold story inside you."

- Maya Angelou

and maybe if i put it down on paper,
i won't have to carry it anymore.

i.

SOIL AND ROOTS

"What you do to children matters. And they might never forget."

- Toni Morrison, God Help the Child

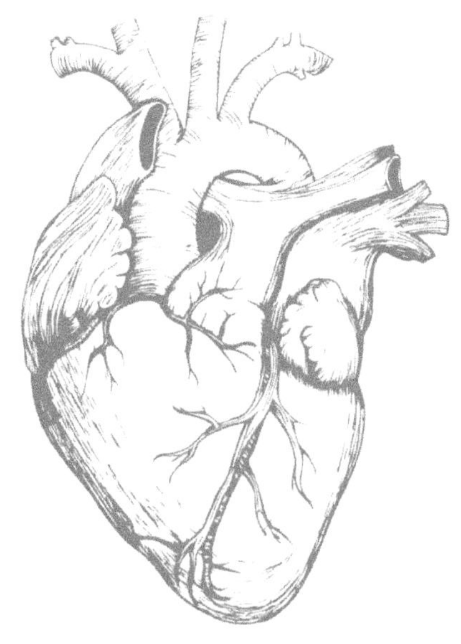

scarred

she was five years young when he began to touch her,
caressing the small, trembling figure as if it were
normal - - good even.
covering her face with a white sheet,
he hovered over her unknowing body,
a breathless dog in heat.
her innocence stolen
by a family member
with a touch that would change her forever.
he gave her love and affection no one had yet shown
if only back then she could have known
that this love was not the only kind;
that the real thing does not trouble the soul or mind.
the sheet no longer a pure white
brought terrors of red at night,
visions of something she could not share,
locked away only for her to bare
on her own for the rest of her years
never able to shed the tears
to mourn for the little girl that is no more
now an empty shell who feels impure
she spends her days in anxiety, dreading
the coming nights, treading
on her last bit of sanity, trying
to block out the voices lying
telling her she's worthless.

inconvenient

don't get in the way
don't be too loud
don't you dare make a mess
make yourself small
and don't say a word
if they see you
if they hear you
you will remind them
of the mistake they made
there's no room for you here
the pain is too thick and
the anger too deep
and the days are too long
and everyone is too tired to remember you
you're what's keeping them here
can't see you see
it's all your fault?

superwoman

i screamed STOP but he didn't hear
he beat me and there was blood
i remember the pink it made with the bath water
and the sound of leather slicing the air
you let him. you knew; but you stayed at work.
then you laughed about it.
i'm still trying to rid myself of the marks it left.
i bleed afresh every time i remember.
why didn't you save me?

my father's footsteps

are thunder and lightning
take the air out of a room
leave no space for exhale
turn my stomach inside out at school
make my brain confuse fight, flight, and freeze
kick my bedroom door open
splash in the puddle of brown drink and broken glass
echo through the house
tell me this is not home.

haven

my teachers don't know
the way my chest becomes abyss
when they threaten to call home,
that for me, fear is spelled d-a-d-d-y
and it consumes me when he shows up,
that i spend the day looking over my shoulder for his shadow.
my teachers don't know
that this classroom is escape,
that i dive into my books to hide
to be anywhere but here,
to disappear
and be
anyone
but me.

mirror, mirror

mirror, mirror on the wall
i'm 13 and my body does not fit in at all.
it's too big, too different, too *grown*
and everyone around me lets it be known.
they ask *what you been doing to get this way?*
i don't know what to say, but i do remember the day
i learned what i see in you is cause for shame,
and the reason i receive so much blame.
they point and say *you better watch her*
as the red in my father's eyes grows darker.

mirror, mirror on the wall
i'm 18 and i am to blame after all.
i kicked, punched, screamed and fought
yet he still continued without a thought.
everyone says *you shouldn't have been there*
and *you need to be more careful with what you wear.*
i wish i could see what they see
and get this target off of me.
i want to crawl out of this skin,
shed the heavy burden of this sin.

mirror, mirror on the wall
i can't stand my reflection
every move i make brings the wrong attention.
no one sees the me of me,
no matter my intention.

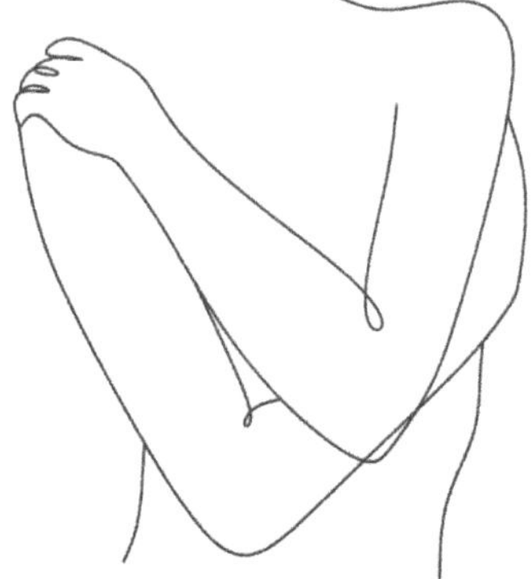

ii.

TELL-TALE HEART

"To love at all is to be vulnerable. Love anything and your heart will be wrung and possibly broken. If you want to make sure of keeping it intact you must give it to no one, not even an animal. Wrap it carefully round with hobbies and little luxuries; avoid all entanglements. Lock it up safely in the casket or coffin of your selfishness. But in that casket, it will not be broken; it will become unbreakable, impenetrable, irredeemable. To love is to be vulnerable."

- C.S.Lewis

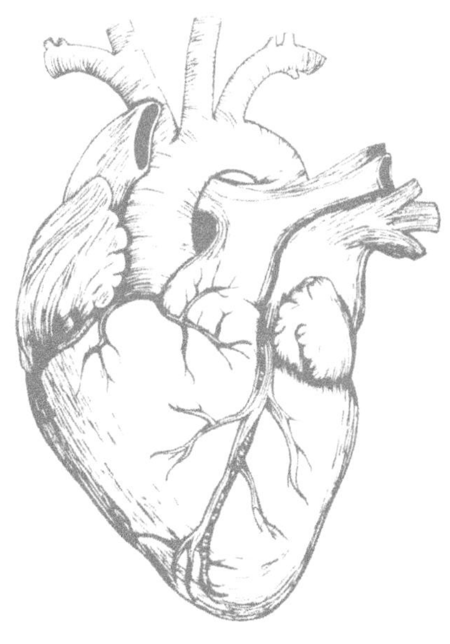

my love is yellow

my love is fast heartbeat and goose bumps,
burning cheeks and tingling spines.
it is long walks to nowhere in particular,
conversations about nothing and everything,
fingers aching to interlock but too shy to reach out.
my love is listening to my favorite songs and
finding you in the lyrics.
my love is hands holding face while
lips greet and fireworks explode behind eyelids.
my love is wobbly knees
and favorite books on rainy days,
stevie wonder on vinyl,
cups of tea and too-big t-shirts.
my love is tangled fingers in hair.
my love is incense and candles,
days in salt water,
trips to the museum.
my love is mario bros. and sonic on gameboy color,
just-because kisses and ugly laughs.
it is donny hathaway and roberta flack,
sir duke and coltrane,
my love is staying up writing,
daydreaming,
hoping,
wishing,
remembering.
-12:17a

daisies in the concrete

when you see the daisies in the concrete, think of me.
think of our endless end, and our forever together.
when you see the daisies in the concrete, listen for me.
listen for whispered i love you's;
listen for my heart beating in time with yours.
when you see the daisies in the concrete,
can you feel me there with you,
wrapping you in my arms and taking you away?
when you see the daisies in the concrete,
remember me
and know that the home you've built in my heart awaits you
know that the deepest parts of me answer to no other call but
yours.
when you see the daisies in the concrete,
remember that the most beautiful flowers grow
out of the hardest places,
and that it takes rain
along with the sunshine
for them to bloom.

14 september

i disconnected our fingers when they accidentally interlocked
because that's not what we were.
i turned off that song that started playing when we were kissing
because that's not what we were.
i stopped you from finishing your sentence that one time
because that's not what we were.
i never told you how i trembled all over from the inside out
on my way to see you
because that's not what we were.
nobody knows we talked all day.
i never held your hand.
i never kissed you the way i wanted to
or touched you the way i wanted to
even though longing persisted
because that's not what we were.
but now i wish i had let my mouth say what my eyes did,
and kissed you from a place i had yet to discover.
i should've poured it all out
so that i wasn't left to bear the burden that is you.
you've left traces of your finger prints on me.
the sound of your laugh still rings in my ears.
i am losing in a war against memories of us,
stuck between bitter and sweet.
smiling at the time we spent together,
grieving because of why it ended,
angry because i can still feel you.
it is impossible to forget you.

time travel

i'm buying a ticket so i can travel back in time
to the place where his heart was so close to mine.
i'd gladly pack my bags and go
and tell myself what i now know.
i'd stay but i wouldn't allow myself to fall
and be sure to keep up an impenetrable wall.
i'm buying a ticket so i can travel back in time
to the place where his heart was so close to mine.
but only a roundtrip it'll be
because his heart doesn't belong to me.
just one more glance, one more sight
of my beloved embodiment of light
is all i need for my trip back to today
where the thought of him never goes away.
i'm buying a ticket so i can travel back in time
to the place where his heart was so close to mine.
when we meet i'll tell him everything i never said,
that he's taken permanent residence in my head,
and the memory of him refuses to move out.
beyond any shadow of doubt,
i'd take our journey's same route
if it meant i could hold him again
the same way i did back then.
i'm buying a ticket so i can travel back in time
to the place where his heart was so close to mine.
i knew he wouldn't be easy to shake
the moment he made my whole being quake
with excitement, pleasure and fear,
for i didn't know how long he'd be here.
i'll be sure to let him know before i leave
that the whole way back to now i'll grieve
for the time together we'll no longer spend
and the heartache from losing a friend.

we'll make time to reminisce
about moments we most miss,
like catching him watching me and blushing,
how it would send blood through my veins rushing,
making belligerent butterflies dance
just from a single graze or glance,
or smiling in the dark when i found it was what it seemed;
he was lying beside me, it wasn't just a dream.
i'm buying a ticket so i can travel back in time
to the place where his heart was so close to mine.
in a perfect world, i'd end our visit and have one last cry
and as i walk away, all the fallen tears would dry.
i'd take back all that i had given,
shared thoughts and feelings i'd kept hidden.
but the world i know is an unfair place
and so now i'm left to face
the cold, unwanted reality:
you and i can't and won't ever be.

untitled

every time the sun rises, i'm reminded of you.
i hope it never sets without you knowing what i feel for you.
and if it does, i'll write it in the sky for you.
i'll have it painted on sky scrapers for you.
i'll whisper things only we know to the wind and hope it finds you
and guides you back to me.
if you should ever forget what you mean to me,
i'd take you to the place where i first loved you
and show you how my heart sighed when it finally found yours.
i'd invite you into the canyons of my mind
and allow you to see yourself the way i do.
if you ever doubt my love for you,
i would allow my hands to tell you of the electric current you sending
coursing through them,
i would let my fingers trace my favorite parts of you,
i would let you hear how our hearts beat in time together,
composing a melody heard only by us and our creator.
and if you're unsure about my devotion to you,
my feet will gladly follow wherever you go.
i keep your secrets written in my heart,
i implore sleep to come
just so i can dream of being yours for the rest of forever
and beyond that.

forget-me-nots

i wish i could uproot the flowers you
planted in my heart
and make room for new ones to bloom.
their scent never leaves.
i pluck their petals,
asking questions i may not want
answers to.
sometimes i water them;
their beauty reminds me of what was.
i long for the day they wither away.

a poem for the sunrise

watch the sun
rise with me.
can we introduce the sun to the new day's beginning of life,
greet her with faces bright and blushing
from the previous night's antics
when we confessed
secrets untold
to the moon and allowed
her light
to cast shadows of our
bodies
saying what our words
could not?
watch the sun

rise
with me.

crime

you come to me with jericho walls
you have no intention of letting down.
i can feel myself begging to let me love you.
loving shouldn't feel like a crime
i've committed
against myself.

an empath's lament

confetti hearts find her
and she answers their call
and opens the door
and all they see is how she can make them feel together again
and when she needs to be seen and heard
they are blind and deaf
they wear their hurt and take it everywhere with them
leaving echoes behind
and she loves them
it hurts
it hurts
it hurts
why did you come here?
just to remind me i don't love me
as much as i love you?
i can
fill
fill
fill
you and want to disappear at the same time.
i want to be empty and numb and cold like they are
but i am full of love for the hurting
a love i can't even give myself
and i feel everything too deeply too much
your hurt is so loud it deafens
so heavy it crushes
so deep it drowns
and something tells me i deserve to suffer it;
i opened the door and let you in.

remember me

don't forget my love.
remember each time i told you you're beautiful
and how it feels to have me wrapped around you.
i wish i could take what i gave you
and wrap it up for safe keeping,
for someone who wants it
for someone who will water it.

now i have to put it away
on a shelf inside me.
maybe one day i'll blow the dust off
and let myself remember
what was
what wasn't.
maybe then it won't hurt
to hear or say your name.

too shy to say (like the stevie wonder song) – part i

if i weren't so afraid of what you'd say back, i'd tell you i love you.
i'd tell you that i trace the veins in your hands while you're asleep.
what i feel is so familiar
like i've always loved you
and time and space were just waiting for me to realize it.

if i weren't so afraid that you don't love me back,
i'd tell you i think you're beautiful,
and that i can't even want anybody but you.
i would tell you that from the time we're apart,
it's like i'm holding my breath
until i see you again.

i can't look you in the eye for fear you'd see
all the things my mouth won't say
that you'd see every dream i've dreamt of you.

i counted your heartbeats until it was blue outside
and i begged the sun not to rise
and end this paradise that felt like home.
i wanted to stay there wrapped in your arms
until the end of forever.

every time my phone lights up, i hope it's you.
i know God is tired of hearing me talk about you,
but your smile is a sunrise and your embrace an exhale.

if i loved you less, i might be able to face you.

too shy to say (like the stevie wonder song) - part ii

i hope these feelings will pour out of me
into these lines
and just stay there.
i love you and i can't tell you.
i want to open up and bloom for you
but i'm scared i won't survive the fall
when you don't catch me.

if you don't love me,
i don't want you to be the last thing i think about at night
or your face to be the first thing I see
before i can even open my eyes
to face another day of not being yours.

i wish i could take my heart
and put it down somewhere,
to not feel it beating for you,
calling out to you
only for you to not hear it.

the first time ever i saw your face: a blackout poem
(song originally by roberta flack)

at last

thank you
for letting me be
every inch
of myself
in every shade
out loud
in the light.

someday

not an hour of any day passes without my mind drawing pictures of my heart's desire to be yours until our bodies are growing flowers. my lips could never form enough thank you's for making real what i've always dreamt of. learning you, growing us, has been the first day of spring after a too-long winter. you see me in all my ugly and still call me beautiful. this is finding the perfect blend in a harmony. this is the perfect bassline to a melody. it feels like the first time i heard my favorite song. every time i look at you, i see forever. to watch you laugh is to see the day break. and even if we don't last to see our bodies fertilize the ground, i love you deep and wide - on purpose.

secret

since i can’t part my lips to say it
or bring myself to tell you to your face
i’ll whisper it to my notebook
and leave this secret between the lines
i love you
i love you
i love you.

i'd have to make up the words,
create new language,
use oceans to measure the depth.
i'd have to borrow time,
and ask God for more,
defy physics,
shrink you to palm size
so i can place you inside my chest
to feel my heartbeat
spelling your name.

- you asked me why i love you

I know I love you because

to swap skin,
dive into tissue,
past bone,
and stay a while.
and there, marrow-deep,
exhale every thought i've thought of you
and let you know that
too close
is impossible.

this is intimacy.

dear God,
i loved him
i love him
but i can't anymore,
can i?

iii.

THIS PRESENT DARKNESS

". . . but the Spirit itself maketh intercession for us with groanings which cannot be uttered."

Romans 8:26

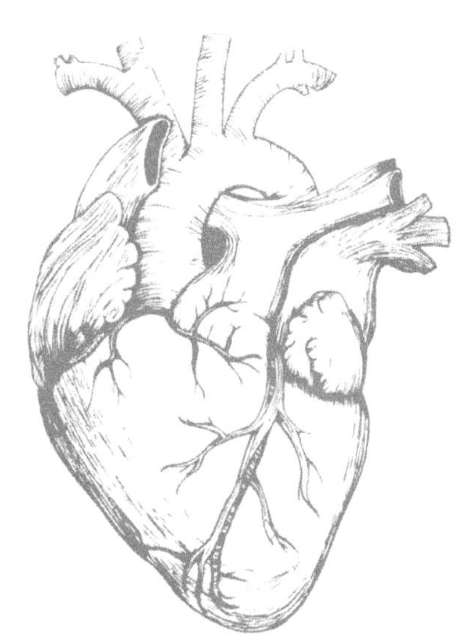

i almost let go.

~~i'm sorry i couldn't take it anymore. i'm sorry i let the darkness win, that i let lies become louder than love. but i was so alone – so alone. i couldn't turn to anyone because they all had solutions i either tried already or was too tired to consider. and i didn't want to hear about what i'd done to cause myself this pain. and i can't pray about it. i've been hurting for as long as i can remember. how much am i supposed to take? how long am i meant to fight what seems so much bigger than me? i have no fight left in me, so i have to go. why stay? i can't do any good here when i can't even move, when everything is so heavy and it's all too loud and the memories are blinding. it's the hopelessness – i don't think i can ever be okay. i've experienced too much and there's so much hurt to heal from. what good can come from such a broken me? i'm not selfish. isn't this mercy? let me go quietly. please just make the pain go away.~~

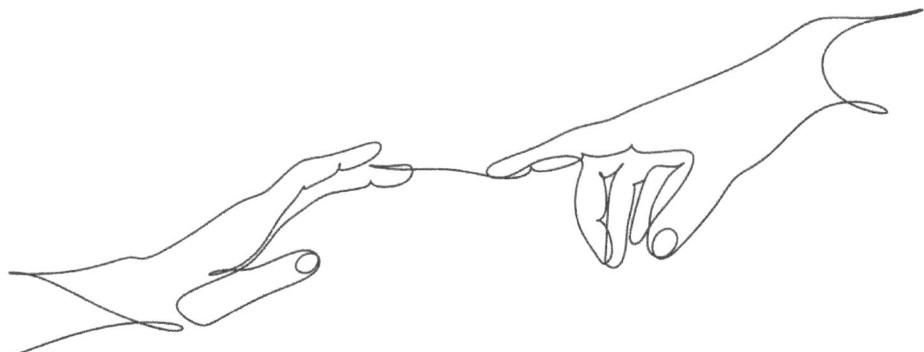

sometimes

sometimes the weight becomes too much
and i ache to join my reflection in the water
sometimes the new day finds me
with 'then sings my soul' on my lips
sometimes i can't outrun the shadows
even in my sleep
but what relief
that troubles don't last

always.

dear God,

please.

free

maybe the Igbo were right
to choose the ocean
over suffering.

the scars on my wrist: a haiku

please don't ask me why.
i wanted to stop hurting.
they tell a story.

I made you and called you good.
I knew you before the bad that happened to you
and the worst that you would do.
it's time to come out of the cave you've made yourself
out of suffocating memories and deafening voices.
step into light.
sit at the table I've prepared.
eat of that which was broken for you.
drink of that which was spilled for you.
rid yourself of what's not yours to bear.
be planted and grow, wither no more.
stand tall as trees, strong as mountains.
My love exceeds oceans' depths,
surpasses what keeps you up at night.
you are made up of the same words that hung stars and moon
and commanded them to give light.

I left the grave for you,
can you leave it for me?

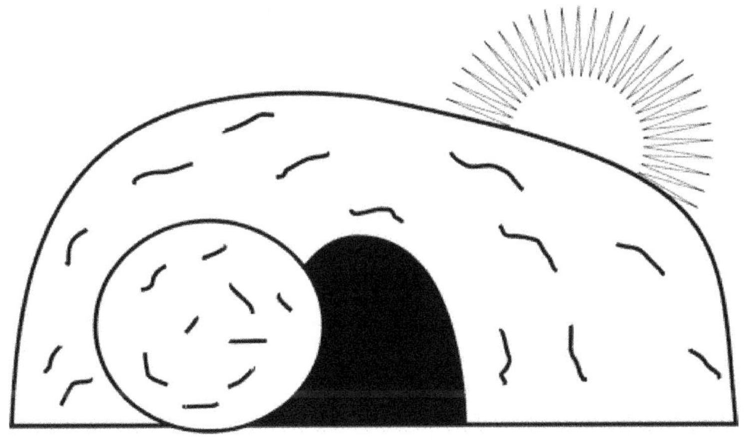

www.ingramcontent.com/pod-product-compliance
Ingram Content Group UK Ltd.
Pitfield, Milton Keynes, MK11 3LW, UK
UKHW051207260726
13967UKWH00011B/3156